The Sin of Craving the Favor of Man

- or -

Thinking Too Highly of the Approval or Disapproval of Man, which is the Fruit of Pride, and a Great Cause of Hypocrisy

- or -

Instructions Against Idolizing Man

A modernized version of Richard Baxter's
"Directions against inordinate Man-pleasing"
from "The Practical Works of Richard Baxter"
London, 1707

by Jon Sharp

Richard Baxter

(November 12, 1615 – December 8, 1691)

Table of Contents

About Richard Baxter

Richard Baxter was born in England at Rowton, Shropshire in 1615, four years after the first King James Bible was published. He was the most prolific writer of his time producing nearly 200 written works, or enough to fill about 60 large volumes. Both of Baxter's parents were laborers so he spent the first ten years of his life living with his grandparents. This, among other situations, resulted in his being largely self-taught, and produced a keen sense of disunity and division in him. He described nearly all of his earliest teachers (mainly the local clergy) as ignorant, illiterate, immoral, infirm or iniquitous. A little later in life his parents undervalued the benefits of education, so for years Baxter simply was not taught. Eventually he was tutored by John Owen at a free school at Wroxeter, where he did fairly well in Latin.

When his progress finally allowed advancement, he set his sights on Oxford University. However Owen advised him not to proceed but instead to tutor with Richard Wickstead, the chaplain to the regional administrative council, at Ludlow. Unfortunately he was tutored half-heartedly and finally persuaded to take the common route to career advancement with a royal court position in London. He quickly forsook the work which he saw as worldly nonsense. Regretting his decision not to proceed to Oxford, he decided to study divinity privately. He was soon ordained into the Church of England as a 23 year-old deacon. Baxter never advanced in the Anglican Church to a position higher than Kidderminster's parish pastor, shepherding loom workers south of Birmingham. This probably didn't discourage him much since he highly regarded the Puritan opposition of the Church's teachings on the historical episcopate.

Though 'only' a parish pastor, Baxter soon became the most prominent English clergyman of the 1600s. His independent study and the effect it had on his often controversial theology, coupled with his great desire for unity among Protestants, brought him into every major controversy in England during his lifetime. He often referred to the old counsel which Philip Schaff called "the watchword of Christian peacemakers:" "In necessary things, unity; in doubtful things, liberty; in all things, charity." Being quite opinionated in his own theology (which varied somewhere between Anglican and Separatist) as well as being a prolific writer, he was called to practice what he preached.

Baxter's extended pastorate at Kidderminster, though broken up by military duty in the English Civil War, was blessed with souls. There was nearly no Christian vitality when he arrived, but his labors in gospel preaching, regular door-to-door visitation, discipleship, catechizing, and pastoral counseling were used by God to save nearly the entire population of 2,000 people, producing a vibrant Christian community.

In 1662 Baxter rejected the Church of England's demands under their *Act of Uniformity* that he must, under oath, reject the Puritan precepts of Church reformation – particularly that the Anglican Church needed to be "purified" of its Roman Catholic-based practices and theology. He refused and was thus ejected from the Church of England. He continued to preach for the rest of his life, but never again pastored a congregation.

At nearly fifty years old Baxter married one of his converts, Margaret Charlton, who was in her early twenties. Due to his fame their age difference caused some controversy, but in time all rumors were silenced by their exemplification of a godly marriage.

Baxter was hounded by clerics and courts for many years. He was imprisoned at least three times for preaching, and all of his books (and once even the bed on which he was lying sick) were confiscated. In 1685, at nearly 70 years old, Baxter was charged with sedition for attacking the Church of England in one of his writings. He was near a death sentence when the Bishop of London intervened. Baxter was spared but was again imprisoned, this time for 18 months. The last four years of his life, except for poor health, were peaceful. He died in London at 76 years old and his funeral was attended by Anglicans and Separatists alike.

Introduction: Instruction against seeking inordinate favor from man

In the case of craving the favor of man and the fear of man, as it is in many other cases, our sin is not simply a cold-hearted neglect of God. This sin is committed when we actively show preference to some rival of God, and when we bow down in subjection to some object which is in opposition to the interest of God. In this case, the rival that we bow down before is man. We therefore assert that anyone who shows any preference for or to man, before or against God, (a) values the favor, acceptance, and approval of man before or against God's approval, and/or (b) fears the condemnation or displeasure of man more than the condemnation or displeasure of God. This is surely a sin of idolatry because the man-pleaser willingly sets a competitor up in God's rightful place and turns his greatest observance, concern, labor, pleasure, and grief toward man, and causes humanity to be the worshipful object of his heart and life, when that object should be God alone. This great and dangerous sin is a common source of much ungodliness, hypocrisy, and pride, and thus requires our scrupulous introspection and attentive watchfulness if we wish to please God.

All creatures, but particularly man, must be regarded and valued only in their proper subordination and subservience to God. If we regard men, their judgments or their acclaim more highly than we regard God, we set man up as God's rivals - and God's rivals are to be despised. The end result of idolatry is the ruin of those that overvalue what (and whom) has been created. See what the Scripture says of this sin:

"Stop regarding man in whose nostrils is breath, for of what account is he?" (Isa 2:22)

"And call no man your father on earth, for you have one Father, who is in heaven." (Matt 23:9)

"But you are not to be called Rabbi, for you have one teacher, and you are all brothers." (Matt 23:8)

"Thus says the LORD: 'Cursed is the man who trusts in man and makes flesh his strength, whose heart turns away from the LORD.'" (Jer 17:5)

"The LORD is on my side; I will not fear. What can man do to me? It is better to take refuge in the LORD than to trust in man. It is better to take refuge in the LORD than to trust in princes." (Psalm 118:6, 8-9)

"I will not show partiality to any man or use flattery toward any person." (Job 32:21-22)

"Am I now seeking the approval of man, or of God? Or am I trying to please man? If I were still trying to please man, I would not be a servant of Christ." (Gal 1:10)

"But with me it is a very small thing that I should be judged by you or by any human court." (I Cor 4:3)

"If anyone comes to me and does not hate his own father and mother and wife and children and brothers and sisters, yes, and even his own life, he cannot be my disciple." (Lk 14:26)

"Blessed are you when others revile you and persecute you and utter all kinds of evil against you falsely on my account. Rejoice and be glad, for your reward is great in heaven, for so they persecuted the prophets who were before you." (Matt 5:11-12)

"Bondservants, obey... not by the way of eye-service, as people-pleasers, but as bondservants of Christ" (Eph 6:6; Col 3:22)

"...just as we have been approved by God to be entrusted with the gospel, so we speak, not to please man, but to please God who tests our hearts." (I Thess 2:4)

"Behold, the Lord comes with ten thousands of his holy ones, to execute judgment on all and to convict all (including those) showing favoritism to gain advantage." (Jude 14-16)

God's Word is clear regarding the snare and sin of seeking inordinate favor from, or giving inordinate deference or respect to man. We must remain vigilant to escape and mortify this sin.

Instruction I: Do Not Run to the Opposite Extreme

We must understand the nature of this sin well to avoid running to the opposite extreme and instead come to know how to plan our resistance to it, therefore we will first examine how far we may regard and please men, when we must regard and please men, and how we must not regard or please men.

The Proper Respect We Are to Have Towards Men

1. Our parents, superiors, authorities, and rulers must be regarded, feared, honored, obeyed, and pleased in all things which they require of us within the several realms of authority which God has given them over us. Furthermore, this must not be done merely as to men, but as to officers of God, from whom, and for whom, (and not against whom) they have all their power (Rom 13; Exo 20:12; Titus 3:1; I Peter 2:13; II Peter 2:10).

2. We must seek to display charity, humility, and gentleness to all men in order to point them to salvation. Our desire to please our Savior should result in such a burden for the conversion of sinners that we labor to become all (lawful) things to all men so that we may save some (I Cor 9:19-23). We must not make our own terms or keep at a distance from them, but instead submit lovingly and contentedly, bearing the infirmities of the weak. To combat apathy we must not take the course that pleases ourselves, but that which, by pleasing God, might edify our weaker brethren. We must be patient with them and forgive them. We must happily lay down our own rights and deny ourselves the use of our Christian liberty, even as long as we live, to point some to their Savior. We must not seek our own worldly goals, but instead the spiritual benefit of others. We must do

them all the good we can by removing any offense which, by their own weaknesses, may harden their hearts (Romans 14:20-21).

3. Jesus' command to love our neighbor requires that we understand the importance of this duty. Because our neighbor is also under the command to love us as himself, we are compelled to make ourselves agreeable to him by all lawful means, in order to help and facilitate his love. Due to his weakness, helping him to love us is more loving than many other ways we might love him. Therefore, if his own depravity causes him to be prejudiced against us, or if some careless word or deed of ours causes him to acquire an aversion for us, we must, as far as we can lawfully, remove the cause of his prejudice and aversion. Yet, he that hates us for obeying God must never be restored by our disobeying God. We have never been called to displease men by quarrelling, gruffness or pessimism. Instead, we are obligated to be kind, patient, and gentle to all with any sort of expression that may be necessary to remedy their sinful hatred or aversion (II Tim 2:24; Phil 4:5).

4. We must not be self-conceited, preferring our own weak, vacuous judgments before the greater wisdom of another; but in honor we must prefer each other. The unlearned and immature must honor the knowledge and qualities in others that excel their own, and not be rigid in their own opinions, or wise in their own eyes. We must not undervalue another man's reasoning or judgment, but instead humbly acknowledge our own insufficiency and be glad to learn from anyone that can teach us.

5. We must especially esteem the judgments of our able, faithful teachers and not set our prideful weaker judgments against them in resisting the truth which they deliver to us from God. It is a

fearful thing to despise the reproofs or admonitions of pastors of the church when they are in line with the word and judgments of God. "Therefore whoever disregards this, disregards not man but God, who gives his Holy Spirit to you." (I Thess 4:8)

Tertullian warns, "If any so offend as to be banished from communion of prayer, and assembly, and all holy matters, it is a judgment preceding the great judgment to come." Indeed, if an officer of Christ, in dealing with matters based on their own perception and judgment, should rebuke you wrongly or by mistake in their desire to maintain righteousness, you must respectfully and patiently bear the wrong so as not to dishonor and despise their authority and office, even though it may have been misused.

6. If prudent, godly persons that are well acquainted with us strongly suspect us to be in sinful error where we do not discern it ourselves, it should cause us to be alarmed and more cautious: and if judicious persons fear you to be hypocrites and unsound Christians when observing your temper, habits and lifestyle, it should cause you to search your heart with a greater scrutiny, and not to disregard their judgment. Conversely, if a godly person (particularly a godly pastor) should tell a poor, fearful, doubting Christian that they believe their spiritual state is safe, it should not be disregarded completely, but should be taken as an encouragement to carry on, even though we cannot take his words as an absolute certainty of their spiritual condition. A godly man's judgment may be valued this far.

7. A good name among men is the reputation of our integrity. It is not to be neglected as insignificant. It is a mercy from God for which we must be thankful, and it is a useful instrument in

successfully serving and honoring God. It may sometimes be a duty (especially for preachers whose work of directing their hearers to salvation depends much on their good name) to vindicate our reputation against some slander in the court of justice. The more respectable we are - and the more the honor of God and faith is connected with our own honor and faith - and the more our reputation will affect the good of men's souls, the more carefully we should guard our reputations.

8. The condemnation and scorn of even our most critical enemies is not to be ridiculed or derided because they are sins that may result in their damnation! Our work is to lament over sin and pray for their redemption. Furthermore, these condemnations may be made very useful in provoking us to a more diligent search of our hearts and careful watchfulness over our ways. Man's judgment may be regarded this far.

- Consider the Nature of Man in General

1. We must, however, realize how frail, erroneous, and fickle man is; and therefore not have too high an expectation from man. We must presume that men will misunderstand us, wrong us, and slander us, whether through ignorance, passion, prejudice, or self-interest. And when this happens we must not think it to be strange or unexpected.

2. We must consider how far unregenerate and ungodly men will take their hostility to holiness and how far the ignorance, prejudice, and passion that is in the ungodly will carry them to despise, scorn, and slander anyone who seriously and zealously serves God. The ungodly will not hesitate to cross us in their worldly interests. Therefore, if for the sake of Christ and righteousness we have all sorts of evil spoken about us falsely, and

we are accounted as scorned, rejected, and malevolent men who instigate rebellion, and are unworthy to live, it must not seem strange or unexpected to us, nor should it dishearten us, but we should instead exceedingly rejoice in hope of our reward in heaven, and bear it all patiently.

3. Considering the remnants of vanity and pride that remain in many that have true grace, and considering how many hypocrites are in the church whose religion consists of their own opinions and their differing modes of worship, we must expect to be reproached and abused by their adversaries and also by them them, even though we do not agree with their opinions, modes, and circumstances. A great deal of injustice, sometimes by slander or reproach, and sometimes by greater violence, must be expected from contentious professors of the same religion as our own, especially when the interest of their faction or cause requires it, and especially if we bring any truth among them which seems new to them, or which crosses the opinions which are established there, or if we would be reformers of them in anything that is amiss.

4. No man must be pleased by sin or desire favor with men before the pleasing of God. Man's favor is in competition with God's, and so it is to be despised. Likewise man's displeasure with our righteousness is to be disregarded. If doing our Scriptural duty displeases them, let them be displeased. We can only pity them.

5. None of our happiness is dependent on the favor or praise of men. We are to account their favor as a matter of unimportance, not worth any great care or endeavor to obtain it, or grief for losing it. We must not only despise it as compared to the approval and favor of God, but we must value it the same as other

passing things. In itself it should be considered as a means to some higher end like the service of God, our own greater good, or another man's greater good. Any further than it contributes to some of these, it must be almost indifferent to us what men think or say of us: and the displeasure of all men, if unjust, must be reckoned with our momentary light afflictions (II Cor 4:17).

6. One truth of God, and even the smallest Christian duty, is to be preferred before the pleasing and favor of all the men in the world. Yet, when it is a means to promote a greater truth or duty, the favor and pleasing of men must be preferred before the uttering of a lesser truth or the doing of a lesser good at that time, because then it is no duty to do it.

7. Our hearts are by nature so selfish and deceitful that when we are being vigilant about protecting our reputation we must carefully watch to prevent our self being intended, and God being pretended. And we must take special care to be sure that we value our own honor and reputation only for the honor of God or the faith, for the good of souls, or for some other benefit greater than self.

8. Man's nature is so prone to go too far in valuing our esteem with men that we should more fear that we will err toward overvaluing it, than toward undervaluing it. And it is far safer to do too little than too much in the vindicating of our own reputation, whether in the court of justice or by disputing or some other contentious means.

9. We must not wholly rest on man's judgment of the state of our souls, nor take their judgment of us as infallible; but use their help that we may more thoroughly examine ourselves.

10. If ministers and councils can err and contradict the word of God, we must do our best to discern it; and after discerning it, we must desert their error rather than the truth of God. As Calvin, and after him David Paraeus, say on I Corinthians 4:3, "We must give an account of our doctrine to all men that require it, especially to ministers and councils: but when a faithful pastor perceives himself oppressed with unrighteous and perverse designs and factions and that there is no place for equity and truth, he ought to be careless of man's esteem, and appeal to God, and fly to his tribunal. And if we are condemned without being able to plead our case and if judgment is passed without our cause being heard, let us turn our minds to God's benevolence, despising men's judgment, and expecting with boldness the judgment of God."

Let us say with Paul, "But with me it is a very small thing that I should be judged by you or by any human court. In fact, I do not even judge myself. For I am not aware of anything against myself, but I am not thereby acquitted. It is the Lord who judges me" (I Cor 4:3-4).

11. God must be enough for the soul of the redeemed, and we must know that "his favor is for a lifetime," (Ps 30:5) and his "steadfast love is better than life," (Ps 63:3) and this must be our concern and labor, that "whether we live or whether we die"(Rom 14:8) we may be accepted by him, and if we have his acceptance it must satisfy us, though all the world condemn us. Therefore, having faithfully done our duty, we must leave the matter of our reputation to God, who, if our ways please him, can make our enemies to be at peace with us, or be as harmless to us as if they were not our enemies. We must quietly leave to God

what measure of wealth and honor we shall have. It is our duty to love and honor, but not to be loved and honored.

12. The prophecy of our Savior must still be believed, that "you will be hated by all" (Matt 10:22), and his example must still be before our eyes, who submitted himself to the point of being spat upon, scorned, buffeted, and slandered as a traitor or usurper of the crown. He "made himself of no reputation" (Phil 2:7-9), and "endured the cross, despising the shame" (Heb 12:2), leaving us an example so that we would follow him, who "committed no sin, neither was deceit found in his mouth. When he was reviled, he did not revile in return; when he suffered, he did not threaten, but continued entrusting himself to him who judges justly" (I Peter 2:22-23). This is what the Christian's usual expectation must be. If we love and follow him, we must not expect to be well spoken of by all, or to have the applause and honor of the world.

13. Not only do the commendations of the ignorant and ungodly have no relevance in eternity; but even the commendations of the most learned and godly must be seen as temporal, so that, when God is pleased to try us in this way, we might bear any harsh criticisms as an easy burden, because our true fulfillment is found in God alone, and in the expectation of his final judgment.

Instruction II. The favor of men is a snare

Remember that the favor, acceptance and approval of man is a snare that will keep you from pleasing God, therefore, watch against the danger of it just as you must do against other earthly things.

Instruction III. Remember that man is only a fellow creature

Remember that even the most venerated man is nothing more than a fellow creature. To revere the favor of a mere mortal is essentially to elevate and revere the creature himself. The approval, acceptance, esteem and commendations of a mortal worm have no eternal value, so why should we imagine that they are of any considerable value to us?

Instruction IV. Remember the judgment of God

Remember how little you are concerned about the judgment of man, and remember that your life or death forever depends only upon the judgment of God alone.

The Judgment of God Compared to that of Man

1. The redeemed soul has been humbled and has felt what it is to have displeased God, and what it is to be under his curse, and what it is to be reconciled to him by the death and intercession of Jesus Christ. He is so consumed by the fear of displeasing God, so preoccupied with seeking the favor of God, and so delighted with his awareness of God's love that he can scarcely bring to mind such a small matter as the favor or displeasure of a man. God's favor is plenty enough for him and so precious to him that, if he finds that it has been poured out upon him, such a small matter as the favor of a man will hardly be missed by him.

2. God alone is our supreme Judge. Our governors are officers that have been appointed by him and whose jurisdiction is limited by him. So if someone should desire to be the ruler, and decides to attempt to set themselves up upon the throne of God, and there lets their condemnations fly upon things and persons which do not concern them, why should we be much concerned about it?

If a beggar should step up into some seat of civil or criminal jurisdiction and begin to fine one person, condemn another, and then turn his attention toward you, will you fear him, or laugh at him? Who is he to judge another man's servant? We stand or fall by the judgment of our own master (Romans 14:4). Men may presume to attempt crossing over the bar of God to judge others according to their own interests and passions: but God will quickly pull them down and teach them better to know their places. How similar is the folly of the world to the games of boys who assemble a pretend jury and appoint a pretend judge to try and condemn one another for amusement! Do we not have a greater Judge to fear?

3. At God's bar He alone passes the final sentence; there is no appeal to any other: yet when judgment is passed by a human there remains an appeal to God. All of man's judgments will ultimately be reviewed and retried by the Supreme Court of God. Things will not stand as men now sentence them. Today, many an evil cause is judged to be good by the multitude or status of those that support it: and many a good cause is now condemned as evil. Many a man is proclaimed to be an evil-doer because he obeys God and does his duty. But all these proclamations will be retried by the Judge that promises "woe to those who call evil good and good evil, who put darkness for light

and light for darkness" (Isa 5:20), and "whoever says to the wicked, "You are in the right," will be cursed by peoples (and) abhorred by nations" (Prov 24:24).

If the judgments of the world against the most holy of Christians would stand, condemning them as fools, hypocrites, and everything else they can think of, then the devil's own judgments would stand. But the wise man is he that, in the end, God judges to be wise; and the happy man is only he that God calls happy.

The erring judgments of sinful man are largely made in ignorance, much like employing an accountant to label the various contents upon an apothecary's shelf. He may very well write 'poison' upon one and 'antidote' on another, but a chemist would never dispense anything according to the labels that the untrained man applied.

How diametric are the labels that God and the world put upon things and persons today! And how many today denounce, despise, criticize, and condemn that which God approves of, and will justify at last! How many will God judge heterodox and wicked that men now judge orthodox and worthy of applause, and how many will God judge orthodox and genuine that were called heretics and hypocrites by men!

God will not verify every word that angry men, or contentious disputants utter against his servants. The worldly education, authority, and other advantages of our opponents may now overwhelm the declarations and reputations of men more wise and righteous than they, but God will restore and vindicate the righteous in the end.

The names of Luther, Zwingli, Calvin, and many other excellent servants of the Lord have been cursed and shamelessly lied about within Roman Catholic writings and reports; but God will judge otherwise, with a more righteous judgment. Oh, how many people and causes the world has condemned! But they will all be justified on the dreadful Day of the Lord! And how many that were justified by the world will be condemned on that Day! It will be a blessed and glorious day to the just, and a day of holy terror to the wicked and every hypocrite. How many things will then be set straight that are now crooked! How many good reputations of innocents and saints were murdered, burned and buried by the world in a heap of lies. Their enemies never imagined that their names, or what's more their bodies, would be revived, yet on that Day they will be resurrected and restored to good standing! O look to that final judgment of the Lord, and you will take men's condemnations as nothing more than the shaking of a leaf.

4. Only God has the power to execute his sentence, to our happiness or misery. "There is only one lawgiver and judge, he who is able to save and to destroy" (James 4:12). If God says to us, "Come you blessed," we can be happy, though devils and men should curse us, for those that he blesses shall be blessed. If God condemns a man to hell, the applause of the world will never fetch him out or give him comfort. A great name on earth, histories written in their applause, or gilded monuments over their bones are poor rewards and no relief to damned souls. All of the barking of the wicked and all of their scorns on earth will never reduce the joy or the glory of the souls that shine and triumph with Christ.

Woe to us if the wicked could execute all their malicious judgments! How many saints would be in hell? But our Lord is the one that "has the keys of death and hell" (Rev 1:18). Please him, and you are sure to escape, though all the wicked ones of the world thunder their most dreadful curses against you. If it is God alone that justifies us, it is an inconsequential matter who on earth condemns us, or what their worldly status may have been! (Rom 8:33)

Instruction V. Would you give honor to the devil?

Remember that the judgments of ungodly men are corrupted and directed by the devil. It is Satan that puts the evil thoughts into the minds of the ungodly, and he puts those reproachful words into their mouths. Would you honor the devil so much by fearing his own empty accusations? To be subjugated by man's judgments, or to fear them too much, is to be subjugated by the devil, and to be afraid of his accusations against us. Even though you would never say you prefer the devil's judgments over God's, to fear the judgments of a man over the judgments of God is equally horrible.

Instruction VI. The favor of man is slavery

Consider the slavery you choose when you make yourselves the servants of every man whose admirations you desire, and whose accusations you fear. "You were bought with a price; do not become bondservants of men" (I Cor 7:23), that is, do not needlessly enslave yourselves1 What an impossible task man-pleasers have! They have as many masters as they have admirers!

No wonder it takes them away from the service of God; for "friendship with the world is enmity with God" (James 4:4). He that is a friend of the world by seeking the favor of man is an enemy to God. He cannot serve both God and the world. He cannot have two masters! (Matt 6:24)

You know men will condemn you if you are true to God: if, therefore, you must have the favor of men, you must take it alone without God's favor. A man-pleaser cannot be true to God, because he is a servant to the enemies of service to God; the wind of a man's mouth will blow the man-pleaser around like chaff, from any duty, and to any sin. How servile a person is a man-pleaser! How many masters he has, and how merciless they are! Man-pleasing perverts the course of sanctification, and turns all from God to this unprofitable way.

Instruction VII. The honor of man is a pitiful reward

Remember what a pitiful reward you seek. "Truly," says our Lord concerning hypocrites and man pleasers, "they have their reward" (Matt 6:25). Oh, what a miserable reward! Instead of God, and instead of heaven, the thoughts and breath of mortal men is their reward! Their happiness will be to lie in hell, and remember that they were well spoken of on earth! -and that once they were accounted religious, learned, wise, or honorable! -and to remember that they preferred this reward before everlasting happiness with Christ! If this is not gain, the labor which you lay out in hunting for applause is all lost. If this is enough to spend your time and energy on, and to neglect your God for, and to lose your souls for, rejoice then in the hypocrite's reward!

Instruction VIII. The acclaim of man is fleeting

Remember that acclaim is found sooner by an honest contempt for it than by seeking it with an inordinate affection of it. It is a shadow which flees from from you if you follow it, and which follows you as fast as you run from it. What names are more honorable upon earth than the prophets, apostles, martyrs, preachers, and holy, mortified Christians who in their days despised the praise of the world? Those godly men were horribly scorned during their days on earth, yet those who sought and were satisfied with the acceptance and approval of their heavenly Father who saw them "in secret" have now been "rewarded by him openly" (Matt 6:18 KJV).

When a man is seen trying to seek out and affect worldly acclaim, he loses it, because an ingratiating desire for man's applause seems a low and pitiful objective, even in the eyes of sinful men. Even they consider living to God above worldly acclaim a far greater honor than seeking man's favor. They would surely ridicule any man who licked up the spittle of every man who spits on the street. Likewise, they will ridicule any man who drinks up their own thoughts and words, and who desires their acclaim and approval more than he thirsts after the God he claims to serve.

Instruction IX. Can you ever please men?

If nothing else will cure this disease, at least let the impossibility of pleasing men and attaining your goals turn you against so fruitless an attempt. And here I shall show you how impossible it is, or, at least, that man-pleasing is a thing which you cannot reasonably expect.

The Folly of Trying to Please Men

1. Remember what a multitude you have to please. When you have pleased some, remember how many more will still remain unpleased, and how many will be displeased even when you have done your best. Alas! We have no way to know how many observe us and may be pleased by us. You are like one that has a few cents in his pocket, and a thousand beggars come to ask him for it, and each one will be displeased if he cannot give to all. If you resolve to give all that you have to the poor, if you do it to please God, you may attain your goal. But if you do it to please them, when you have pleased those few that you gave it to, it's likely that twice as many will revile or curse you because they received nothing. The beggar that is quick will proclaim you generous, and the beggar that is slow will proclaim you greedy and unmerciful. You will have more to offend and dishonor you than to comfort you by their praise, if pleasing man must be your comfort.

2. Remember that all men are so selfish that their expectations will be higher than you are able to satisfy. They will not consider your occupations, or hobbies, or what you do for others. Most of them look to have as much of your time as if you had nobody else to mind but them. Many times, when I have had an hour or a day to spend, a multitude of people have each expected that I should have spent it with them. When I visit one, ten more are offended that I am not visiting them at the same hour: when I am having a conversation with one, many more are offended that I am not speaking to them all at once. If those that I speak to account me

courteous, humble, and respectful, those that I could not speak to, or but in a word, account me discourteous and bad-tempered. How many have rebuked me, because I have not allowed them the time which God and conscience commanded me to spend upon greater and more necessary work! If you have any office to give, or benefit to bestow which only one can have, each one thinks he is the most deserving; and when you have pleased the one that got it, you have displeased all that failed to get what they desired.

3. You will have a multitude of people to please that are so ignorant, unreasonable, and weak, that they take your greatest virtues for your faults, and do not know when you do well or poorly; and yet none are more bold in rebuking than those that least understand the things they rebuke. Many men's sermons have been judged and openly defamed for that which never was in them, due to the ignorance or thoughtlessness of a critical hearer; indeed many sermons have been criticized because they were simply not understood. The most able speakers are the most frequently misreported.

4. You will have many contentious zealots to please, who being strangers to the love of holiness, Christianity, and unity, are ruled by the interest of an opinion or a sect; and these will never be pleased by you unless you join their side or party and conform yourself to their opinions. If you are not against them, but set yourselves up to reconcile and end the differences in the church, they will hate you for not promoting their opinions, and claim that you weakened them by some detestable syncretism. Ecclesiastical wars are similar to civil wars in that the passionate cannot endure the peaceable. If you are neutral, you will be seen as an enemy. It means nothing to them for you to be passionate

about Christ, holiness, and common truth, unless you are also for them and their notions.

5. Because they are not renewed by the Holy Spirit, most of the world hates holiness, and has a satanic opposition to the image of God. They will not be pleased with you unless you will sin against your Lord, and do as they do. "For the time that is past suffices for doing what the Gentiles want to do, living in sensuality, passions, drunkenness, orgies, drinking parties, and lawless idolatry. With respect to this they are surprised when you do not join them in the same flood of debauchery. They malign you, but they will give account to him who is ready to judge the living and the dead" (I Peter 4:3-5). If you tell them of their sin you will be compared to Lot among the Sodomites, a busybody that comes among them to make himself their judge and to control them. If you abstain from their sinful activities and will not do as they do in their sensuality and contempt of God (though you say nothing), you are seen as finger-pointer and will be called rigid, hypocritical, and conceited (or perhaps much worse). Among the insane you must act insane if you want to escape the fangs of their castigations. Can you hope to please such men?

6. You will have malicious, cruel, satanic God-haters and men of seared and desperate consciences to please. They will be pleased with nothing but some horrid iniquity, the damning of your own souls, and drawing others to damnation. This is like that monster of Milan, who, when he had brought down an enemy, made him blaspheme God in hopes of having his life spared, but then stabbed him, calling it a noble revenge that killed the body and damned the soul at once. There are some in the world that will shamelessly play the devil's part in order to lead believers astray

and pollute their consciences with horrid deceitfulness, faithlessness, and blasphemies. If you think it is worth the willful damning of your souls it may be possible to please them. But if you tell them "we cannot please you unless we will be dishonest, and displease God, and sin against our knowledge and consciences, and hazard our salvation," they will make a joke of your arguments and, caring little for God and your souls, expect you to gamble your souls and eternity upon their opinions. Desperate sinners are not happy to go to hell alone; it torments them to see others as better than themselves. Those who are cruel and unmerciful to themselves, and have no pity on their own souls, will sell their souls for a whore, special treatment, honor, or other sensual delights. It is highly unlikely that they will have any mercy on the souls of others: "His blood be on us and on our children!" (Matthew 27:25)

7. You will have harsh, critical, uncharitable, and unrighteous men to please, who "by a word make a man out to be an offender, and lay a snare for him who reproves in the gate, and with an empty plea turn aside him who is in the right" (Isa 29:20-21), that will have none of that charity which covers faults and interprets words and actions favorably, or that justice which causes men to do as they would have done to them, and judge as they would hope to be judged. But by judging without mercy, they are likely to face judgment without mercy. They are glad when they can find anything that might disgrace you: and once they find it (true or false) they will never forget it, but dwell on it like a fly on an ulcerated wound.

8. You will have many people to please whose judgments are blinded because they are prone to anger. Like those who are ill that are hurt with every touch, Seneca says "they are only weak

creatures that think themselves wounded if they be but touched." How can you please the angry ones when displeasure is the disease that plagues their very heart?

9. You will find that criticism is a common vice. Few are competent judges of your actions because they can never know the entire case that led to your choices, yet nearly everyone will attempt to register a complaint against you at some point. A proud, presumptuous understanding is also a very common vice which thinks itself capable of judging as soon as it hears even a small piece of the case, and it is not conscious of its own fallibility even though it daily experiences it. Few people in your life are constantly by your side, and none are in your heart, therefore they can never know the circumstances and reasons of all that you do. It is rare, even among the most sincere church people, to meet anyone who is sensitive, mindful, and fearful of sinning by the careless, groundless judgments they speak without first having full comprehension or good reason. They never know all of your reasons for all that you do, yet they will presume to accuse you - even though they surely would have exonerated you if they had only heard you explain your actions.

10. You live among troublemakers, tattlers, and tale-bearers that desire to please others by accusing you. Though there are a few upright men whose somber countenance has driven away such back-biting tongues, there are few ears that are not infested with such busy vermin as these earwigs. Everything they have to say about you will be said behind your backs when you are incapable of answering for yourselves. And if he that accuses or back-bites you is a man that the hearers respect, they will think it acceptable to believe them. Indeed they will consider most of their friends to be honest - and therefore credible - since they share their

interests and beliefs. It is human nature for an educated, intelligent, or even godly person, to be ready to repeat an evil report from the mouth of another. The hearer then thinks he is fully justified for listening to it, believing it, and reporting it again to others, simply because of who spoke it. Even David himself, by the temptation of a Ziba, was drawn to do wrong to Mephibosheth, the son of his great, deserving friend (2 Sam 16:3). No wonder then that Saul summoned Doeg to murder the priests after his false report about David. "The words of a whisperer... go down into the inner parts of the body" (Prov 18:8). "For lack of wood the fire goes out, and where there is no whisperer, quarreling ceases" (Prov 26:20). As long as there are still men nearby to tell, and as long as you are far away, it is easy for a troublemaker to perpetuate the most offensive representations of the actions of even the most admirable person in the world.

11. The fallibility of all men in understanding and godliness is so great, that differences in judgments among the best of them will still result in injuring and disparaging their brethren. One man is confident that his way is right, and another is confident of the contrary. We will never know in this age the great contentions and injuries such differences have preceded. We have no need to go to Paul and Barnabas for an instance (that was a far lighter case); nor to Epiphanius, Jerome, and Chrysostom; nor to those times and tragedies of the contending churches during the Reformation. Every man thinks his cause is so plain that he will justify himself in all that he says and does against those that presume to differ with him. And surely you too should expect some displeasure, even from good and learned men, when the Church has for so many years felt the dreadful buffetings of these

horrid divisions. She bleeds to this day since many of her leaders still harbor remnants of that same arrogance and ignorance.

12. You will have men of great inconsistency to please. One hour they may be ready to worship you as gods, and the next to stone you, or account you as devils, as they did to Paul, and even Jesus himself. The mind of man, especially of the carnal and hypocrite, is like a weather vane, ever changing with the climate! If you spend your days building your reputation on these shifting sands, one blast of wind or storm will tumble it down, and all of your cost and labor will be lost in the end. Even when you serve men as submissively and carefully as you can, some accident or failure to meet their unrighteous expectations may make them forget all that you ever did. After trying to bring some reform to the Roman Catholic Church, Cardinal Thomas Wolsey was accused of treason and sentenced to death, but his long journey from Yorkshire to the Tower of London did the work of the executioner early. Just before he died he groaned, "If I had served God as diligently as I have done the King, he would not have given me over in my grey hairs." Many have fallen by the hands or scowls of men whose favor had been purchased by them at great price - perhaps at the price of their salvation! If you ever put such confidence in a friend that you consider it impossible that he may one day prove to be your enemy, you do not know man. Your time to get to know man better might then be to your great loss.

13. Every living man will unavoidably be engaged by God himself in some duties which are very likely to be misconstrued, and which will be offensive to sinful man, and which will have an appearance of evil to some who do not know all of the details and circumstances. This is why it has come to pass that a great part of

written history is not worthy of much regard because the recorded actions of public people were understood only by the part of the story available to the writers. In these cases they wrote mostly by hearsay, or knew only the outward appearance of things, and not the spirit, life, and reality of the case. Men are not able to choose their own duties, but God establishes them by his law and providence, and it pleases him often to try his servants in this way. Many of the circumstances of the actions of godly men will remain unknown to men that would justify them if they knew them. So instead they account them as notorious, scandalous persons because they did not know them. The Israelites taking the goods of the Egyptians was quite similar in appearance to evil. It was in obedience to God, but was very likely to subject them to derision! Likewise with Abraham's intention to sacrifice his son: and David's eating the shew-bread; and his dancing in his humble attire before the ark; and Christ's eating and drinking with publicans and sinners; and Paul's circumcising Timothy and purifying in the temple. There are many similar examples which occur in the life of every obedient Christian. No wonder Joseph once thought of putting Mary away - until he knew the evidence of her miraculous conception! How prone she was to ridicule by those that did not know the full story! The judgments of man are so defective and frequently contrary to the truth that any history must be read with great caution! Oh, how glorious the great Day of the Lord will be, when all human condemnation shall be justly condemned!

14. The perverseness of man is so great that what they demand, in order to be pleased, is impossible to provide. They are resolved to never be pleased by you. When John does not eat or drink they say, "He has a devil." When Jesus does eat and drink they say,

"Look at him! He is a glutton and a drunkard, a friend of tax collectors and sinners!" (Matt 11:18-19) Even the most righteous man will never please men.

When you try to conform your thoughts and actions to what man demands, especially if you have admitted a change of mind, you will be judged untrustworthy and an equivocator: when you do not, you will be judged disobedient, obstinate, and seditious. If you speak fairly and pleasingly, they will call you a flatterer and a grandstander: if the case necessitates that you speak more frankly, they will say you berate. If you accept some preferential treatment they will say you are ambitious, proud, and worldly: if you refuse it, (regardless of how modestly) they will say you are antagonistic and a rebel. If you do not preach when you are forbidden to do so, you will be accused of forsaking your calling - and obeying man against God; if you do preach, you will be called disobedient and seditious. If a friend or relative asks you to give him a reference for some promotion, even if he replaces one who failed in his duties, you will be accused of doing wrong to another by your partiality; if you refuse to do so, you will be called unfriendly or accused of disloyalty and called worse than an infidel. If you give to the poor as long as you have it, you shall be disparaged when you cease, even though you have no more to give. Those who do not know whether you have it to give or not will be displeased if you do not give; and if you continue giving freely for many years, it will be as if you gave nothing as soon as you cease because your supply has been spent, or because it has become necessary to make someone else the object of your charity. If you go to court when you are wronged in your estate, they will say you are contentious; if you give up your estate to avoid contention they will say you are a silly fool or an idiot. If you do any charitable deed to the knowledge of men, they will say you are a hypocrite and do it for applause; if you do it secretly so that no one knows about it, they will say you are covetous and do no good deeds. Furthermore, others will be blamed for what you do or do not do. If you are pleasant and merry, they will accuse you of being light and vain: if you are more solemn and sad, they will say you are melancholy or discontent. In a word, whatever you do you can be sure it will be condemned by someone. And whether you do or not do, speak or be silent, you will certainly displease somebody. You will never escape the disapprovals of the world.

15. Among men there are so many contradictions and differences in judgments, dispositions, and interests that they will never agree among themselves; and if you please one, the rest will be displeased by it. He that you please is an enemy to another therefore you displease his enemy by pleasing him. Sometimes politics divide people, parties, states or nations into factions and one faction will be displeased with you if you belong to the other, and both will be displeased if you are neutral or dislike them both. Each faction thinks their cause will justify any accusations they hurl at you, or justify the most detestable names they call you (when they cannot bring any other sufferings upon you). Church differences and sects have been found in every age, and you cannot be of the opinion of every party. The world abounds with a great variety of notions, and you cannot align with all of them at once. If you are of one party you must displease the rest; if you are of one side in opposing opinions, the other side will say you are in error: and the supposed interest of their cause and party will have them defend it to their death! One half of the Christian world today condemns the other half as being

schismatic at least, and the other half does the same. Can you be Roman Catholic, and Protestant, and Greek Orthodox, and every other thing at the same time? If not, you will displease as many as you please. What's more, when fickle men change they will expect that you change as fast as they do, and demand that you follow them in whatever their contrary interests require. One year you must swear, and the next year you must renounce all that you swore. You must approve of whatever devilish cause or action they engage in, accept it, and say that all they do is well done. In a word, you must teach your tongue to say or swear anything, and you must sell your innocence, and hire out your consciences wholly to their service, or you cannot please them. Micaiah must say with the rest of the prophets, "Go, and prosper," or else he will be hated for prophesying evil to Ahab instead of good (I Kings 22:8).

How can you serve all interests at once? The providence of God has purposed to turn the affairs of the world backwards in order to shame and reveal the man-pleasers and equivocators. It is evident then, that if you will please all you must at once both speak and be silent, and verify contradictions, and be in many places at once, and be of all men's minds, and for all men's ways. For my part, I will wait to see the world a little better agreed among itself before I will make it my ambition to please them. You might possibly have a hope of pleasing them only when you can reconcile all their opinions, interests, complexions, and dispositions, and make them all of one mind and will.

16. So unreasonable are malicious men that you will not be excused from their contrary defamation even if you excel in any one virtue or duty. Nothing in the world will secure you from censorious, slanderous tongues. The perfect holiness of Jesus

Christ did not keep him from being called a gluttonous person and a wine-bibber, and a friend of publicans and sinners. His complete rejection of worldly dignities and honors and his subjection to Caesar did not keep him from being slandered and crucified as Caesar's enemy. The great piety of the ancient Christians did not save them from the profane accusations of their slanderers who said that they met together for filthiness in the dark. Their godly stance against the worshipping of idols did not quiet the cry of the mobs who said; *"Tollite impios! Away with the ungodly!"* Some have given all that they ever had to the poor except their food and necessaries, and though they gave a considerable amount to some, they were reproached as being unmerciful when some did not receive what they expected. Many who have lived in untainted chastity all their lives have been defamed with scandalous rumors of uncleanness. The most eminent saints have been defamed as guilty of the most horrid crimes which never entered into their thoughts. The principal thing that I have bent my studies and concerns around has been the reconciling, unity, and peace of Christians against disunity, unkindness, disorder, and division; and yet the interest and malice of some have brought them to charge me with the very sin against which I have spent my days, zeal, and study. How often have opposing factions charged me with equally opposing accusations! I can hardly think of anything in the world that I can do that some will not be offended by; nor a duty, no matter how great and clear, that some will not say is my sin; nor a holy self-denial (even to the hazard of my life) that some will not say is self-seeking; or something righteous that some will not say is the complete opposite of what it actually was. Therefore, instead of serving and pleasing this malicious, unrighteous world, we must reject their blind and unjust criticisms, and appeal only to the most righteous God.

17. If you have hopes for a name of honor when you are dead, consider what power a prevailing faction may have to corrupt the history of your life, representing you to posterity perfectly contrary to what you are. Consider how impossible it is for posterity to know whose history is the product of malicious, shameless lies, and whose is the narrative of impartial truth. There are many contrary histories about particular persons and actions written by men of the same religion, like that of Pope Gregory VII and the emperors that contested him; and about Pope John, and many similar cases, where you may read scores of historians on one side and on the other.

18. Remember that none of the holiest saints, apostles, or even Jesus Christ himself, ever pleased the world or escaped their condemnations, slanders, and cruelties. Do you think you will please them better by honest means than Jesus and all his saints have done? You do not have the wisdom, perfect innocence, and blamelessness that Christ had to please men and to avoid offense. You cannot heal their sicknesses and infirmities or do such good to please and win them as Jesus could. You cannot convince them, and compel them to reverence you by manifold miracles, as Jesus did. Can you imitate such an excellent example as has been set by the holy, patient, charitable, unwearied apostle Paul? (Acts 20; I Cor 4, 9; II Cor 4, 5, 6, 10, 11, 12) If you cannot, how can you please those who would not be pleased by such inimitable works of love and power? The more Paul loved some of his hearers, the less he was loved (II Cor 12:15). He became their enemy for telling them the truth (Gal 4:16). Though he "became all things to all people" so he could "save some," he still

also displeased some (I Cor 9:22). Who are you that you might better please them than Paul?

19. Godliness, virtue, and honesty itself will never please the world therefore you cannot hope to please them by that which is not pleasing to them. Will men ever be pleased by that which they hate or by the actions which they think accuse them and condemn them? And if it requires that you be ungodly and vicious to please them, then you sell your soul, your conscience, and your God, to please them. God and men are not pleased with the same ways. Whom do you think should first be pleased? If you displease God for their favor, you will pay for it dearly. Is it worth the price?

20. Can you do more than God to please them? Or can you deserve their favor more than he? They are not pleased with God himself. Indeed, no man displeases so many or as much as God. They are daily displeased with his works of providence. One would like rain, when another would like none. One would like wind to serve his voyage while another wishes the wind would stop. One party is always displeased because another is pleased. Every enemy wants his cause to succeed and to gain the victory, and every contender wants the same for his side. They will not be pleased with God until he is ruled by them and bends his holy will to the will of the most unjust and the most vicious, doing as they would have him do, and being a servant to their lusts. And God's holy nature, and his holy word, and his holy ways displease them far more than his ordinary providence. They are displeased that his word is so explicit and severe, and that he commands such a holy and strict life, and that he threatens all the ungodly with damnation. Before they will be pleased with God's commands (unless he alters their minds and hearts) he must alter

his laws and make them more loose, and fit them to their carnal interests and lusts, and speak as they would have him speak without any difficulties. How do you think they will be pleased with him at last when he fulfils what he has threatened, when he kills them, and turns their bodies to dust, and delivers their guilty souls to torment and despair in hell?

21. How can you please men that cannot even please themselves? Their own desires and choices will only please them a little while, like children who are soon weary of that which they cried for. They demand to have it, and when they finally have it they do not want it any longer and throw it aside. They are not pleased without it or with it. They are like a sick person that longs for meat and drink, and when they have it they cannot get it down because of the sickness that is still within them. How many trouble and torment themselves day to day by their passions and folly! Could you possibly please anyone that can't even please themselves?

22. How can you please all others when you cannot please yourselves? There will be no one in the world as displeasing to you as you are to yourselves if you have come to fear God, feel the burden of your sins, and be alive enough to be sensible of your disease. You carry with you, and feel within you, the sin which displeases you more than all the enemies you have in the world. Your passions and corruptions, lack of love for God, strangeness to him and to the life to come, and the daily faultiness of your duties and your lives, are your daily burden and they are most displeasing to you. If you are not able, wise, or good enough to please yourselves, will you be able, wise, or good enough to please the world? Just as your sin is nearest to yourselves, so are God's graces; and just as you know more evil about yourselves than

others know, so too you know more good about yourselves. A little fire that will not warm the hearth it lies upon will certainly never warm all the room.

Instruction X. Seeking favor from men brings wearying frustration

Remember what a life of unrest and continual frustration you choose if you place your peace or happiness in the good will or word of man. Having showed you how impossible a task you undertake it must follow that the pursuit of it will be a life of torment. To engage yourselves in such difficult labors when you are sure to be disappointed; to make approval of men your goal which you cannot attain; to find that you daily labor in vain only to meet with displeasure instead of the favor you expected; this will be a very grievous life. You will be like a man that dwells on the top of a mountain, and yet cannot bear to have the wind to blow upon him; or like him that dwells in a forest, and yet is afraid of the shaking of a leaf. You dwell among a world of diseased, selfish, contradictory, fickle, unpleasable minds, and yet you cannot endure their displeasure.

Are you a pastor or teacher? You will seem too rough to one, and too smooth to another. Indeed, you will be too rough and too smooth to the same man when you reprove him or call his faults into his view and also stand as a friend to sinners. No sermon that you preach is likely to be pleasing to all your hearers; nor any of your ministerial works.

Are you a judge? If so, the people will murmur at you, and those that are most incompetent and incapable will be the first to condemn you, and think that they could govern much better than you. Those that bear the necessary burdens of civil safety and defense will say that you oppress them, and the criminals that are punished will say you deal with them unmercifully, and those that have an unjust cause will say you have wronged them if the case does not go their way.

Are you a lawyer? The clients that lost their case will call you unscrupulous behind your backs, and say you betrayed them. And those that prevailed will call you covetous and tell how much money you took them for, and how little you did for it. You should not be amazed that among the worldly your profession is the matter of their reproach.

Are you a doctor? You will be accused of being guilty of the death of many that die; and as covetous takers of their money whether the patient lives or dies. This is the common talk of the world, except with those few with whom your honor-seeking has much succeeded, and then only for some time.

Are you a business man? Most men that buy from you are so selfish that, unless you put yourselves in financial ruin, they will say you deceive them and deal unscrupulously and sell too high. They care very little about the necessary maintenance of your families, nor whether you live or profit by your trading. If you will go into arrears to make them a good deal they will say you are very honest men. Yet when you are insolvent they will accuse you of recklessness and of defrauding your creditors. You must buy high and sell low and live by the loss, or else displease men.

Instruction XI. Remember your true business

Remember that pleasing God is your primary business in the world, and that only in pleasing him will your souls have safety, rest, and full content, even though the entire world might be displeased with you. God is enough for you; and his acceptance, favor and approval is your portion and reward. How sweet and safe is the life of the faithful and upright ones that study more to be righteous than to seem righteous, and who think that if God accepts them that they have enough! O what a mercy is an upright heart which renounces the world and all in the world that stands in competition with his God.

The upright heart takes God for his God and his Lord, Judge, and Portion as well. In temptation the upright heart remembers the eye of God. In all his duty he is animated and ruled by the will and pleasure of his Judge and regards the eye and thoughts of man only as he would regard the presence of a bird or beast unless piety, justice, or charity requires him to have respect to man in due subordination to God.

The upright heart of a person of excellent holiness and goodness will be watchful and concerned when he is applauded by men, desiring to make sure that the all-knowing God doesn't think otherwise of him than his applauders. The upright heart can live in peace with the acceptance of his God alone, and can rejoice in his justification by our righteous Judge and gracious Redeemer, even under the petty accusations, reproaches, slanders, and condemnations of evil men (or even when good men might be tempted to abuse him in that way.)

How can any but upright hearts live a life of true, lasting peace and joy? If God's acceptance, favor, and approval do not bring you peace and joy, nothing can rationally bring it to you. If pleasing God does not satisfy you even when men, - even when good men, - even when all men, - are displeased with you, how or when do you imagine you will be satisfied?

You will have a much more even, contented, quiet life when you disregard the judgments and displeasure of the profane, and when you do not disregard the judgments and displeasure of the godly when God is pleased to use them to try you, as he did with Job's wife and friends.   We will now consider:

The Advantages of Pleasing God Rather than Men

1. If you seek first to please God, and are satisfied in so doing, you have just one to please instead of multitudes. A multitude of masters are harder to please than one.

2. There is only one master that burdens you with nothing that is unreasonable, in quantity or quality.

3. There is only one master that is perfectly wise and good, and not liable to misunderstanding your case and actions.

4. There is only one master that is most holy and not pleased by iniquity or dishonesty.

5. There is only one master that is impartial, most just, and no respecter of persons (Acts 10:34).

6. There is only one master that that has the authority, competence, and qualifications to judge, and is acquainted with your hearts, and every circumstance and reason of your actions.

7. There is only one master that perfectly agrees with himself, and does not burden you with contradictions or impossibilities.

8. There is only one master that is constant and unchangeable, and is not pleased with one thing today, and another contrary thing tomorrow; or pleased with one person this year, that he will be weary of the next.

9. There is only one master that is merciful, and does not require you to hurt yourselves to please him. Indeed, he is pleased with nothing of yours but that which tends to your happiness, and displeased with nothing but that which hurts yourself or others, as a father that is displeased with his children when they corrupt or hurt themselves.

10. There is only one master that is gentle yet just in his rebukes, judging truly, but not with unjust harshness, nor judging your deeds to be worse than they are.

11. There is only one master that is not subject to the passions which blind the minds of men and carry them to injustice.

12. There is only one master that cannot be bent by any misinformation, nor influenced by tale-bearers, whisperers, or false-accusers.

The Benefits of Seeking to Please God

Consider also the benefits of making it your goal to please God rather than man.

1. The pleasing of God is itself your happiness. It is the source of a pure, full and constant comfort which you can always have

nearby, and which no man can take from you. Get this comfort and the work of pleasing man will become more and more unappealing. Nothing can add to that wonderful comfort except the perfecting of it when we enter our eternal rest in heaven.

2. When pleasing God is your prime endeavor, you will escape an abundance of disappointments and wearying frustrations which tear at the very hearts of man-pleasers, filling their lives with unprofitable sorrows!

3. When pleasing God is your prime endeavor, your cares, desires, thoughts, and labors will be ordered and led to their right and proper end, preventing the perverting of them, so that they will not be wasted in sin and vain regard for the approval of the creature over the Creator.

4. When pleasing God is your prime endeavor, it will not only make your life more holy, but it will make such a sanctified life to be sweet and easy, because you disregard the human reproach which would create prejudice and difficulties in you. While others glory in wit, wealth, and strength, you glory in this; that you know the Lord (Jer 9:23-24).

5. When pleasing God is your prime endeavor, you will not only increasingly reject the inordinate esteem of man (because you understand that God alone is worthy of such esteem), but you will also increasingly show proper respect toward God. This is indeed to walk with God, and it will deeply affect your heart and life.

6. When pleasing God is your prime endeavor, you will begin to see the accumulation and compounding of God's graces in your life. Faith, humility, love, holy desire, trust, the fear of God, and

contentedness will increase and blend together as you succeed in your endeavor. "The LORD of hosts, him you shall honor as holy. Let him be your fear, and let him be your dread" (Isa 8:13).

7. "When a man's ways please the LORD, he makes even his enemies to be at peace with him" (Prov 16:7). It is God that appropriates human regard for his people by appeasing the wrath of men, or by restraining them from their intended evil, or by using what they intend for our harm to work out for our good. If human regard might ever be worth having and good for you, then pleasing God is the best way to procure it.

The Signs of Living to Please God

See to it then, that you live your life primarily seeking God's approval as that which satisfies you. The following are evidences that you are doing so:

1. You will increasingly strive to know and understand the Scriptures, "rightly handling the word of truth" (II Tim 2:15) both to know God, and thereby, to know what pleases and displeases God.

2. You will increasingly be more vigilant in doing every duty, to ensure that God, rather than man, is pleased with you.

3. You will increasingly examine your heart, motives and thoughts, and the inward ways and degrees to which they will be pleasing (or displeasing) to God.

4. You will increasingly examine your public deeds, desiring to please God in that which men see, and you will increasingly

examine your secret deeds, desiring to please God in that which men do not see.

5. You will increasingly respect your Holy Spirit-enabled consciences, and pay attention to them, and not offend them. When they warn you of God's displeasure it will alarm you, and when they intimate his approval it will comfort you.

6. When men are, for some reason, pleased with you, it will increasingly be rooted in your godly desire for their spiritual good, and you will increasingly be sanctified in your ongoing desire to be pleasing to God; less and less proud and ambitious for honor with men, and less and less unfaithful in pleasing God.

7. You will increasingly consider it to be of little importance to you whether men are pleased or displeased with you, or how they judge you, or what they call you, because their own opinions are a small matter in comparison to God's judgment. Your life does not rely on their pleasure. If God is pleased with you, you can bear the displeasure, condemnations, and reproaches of men.

THE END

This is the First Volume in a Series:
Dead Guys Modernized

www.vertigocreative.com/deadguys

Printed in Great Britain
by Amazon

28232068R00031